EMPATH

THE SURVIVAL GUIDE FOR HIGHLY SENSITIVE PEOPLE

Author
Amalia Elle

Copyright © 2018 Amalia Elle
All rights reserved.

About the book

We all can be empathetic, but being an Empath is a rare gift. Empaths are people who put others before themselves. Showing empathy can simply be imagining how it feels like to be in someone's position, but an Empath can literally bring himself to that place and use all his mental energy in realizing the other person.

In this book, we are going to focus not only on empathy as a skill but on Empaths. It is a survival guide including life hacks to develop, survive and sustain being an Empath, what challenges they face and how they can overcome the hurdles of an Empath life.

CONTENT

INTRODUCTION	7
UNDERSTANDING EMPATHY THE DIFFERENCE BETWEEN EMPATH AND EMPATHY	9
QUALITIES OF AN EMPATH	14
ARE YOU AN EMPATH?	16
10 SIGNS THAT YOU ARE AN EMPATH	18
TYPES OF EMPATH	19
THE SELF-HELP TEST FOR EMPATHS	21
EMPATHY SPECTRUM	24
SCIENTIFIC THEORIES RELATED TO EMPATH AND EMPATHY	28
THE THEORY OF ELECTROMAGNETIC FIELDS –	29
THE DOPAMINE HYPOTHESIS THEORY –	30
HOFFMAN'S EMPATHY THEORY –	31
SIMULATION THEORY OF EMPATHY	33
LIVING LIFE AS AN EMPATH NUGGETS TO EMBRACE YOUR EMPATH GIFT	34
HOW DOES BEING AN EMPATH FEELS	35
TIPS TO EMBRACE YOUR EMPATH GIFT	36
GROWING AS AN EMPATH	38
CONTROL YOUR EMPATH ABILITIES	40
CONTROLLING EMPATH ABILITIES --WHY IS IT IMPORTANT TO CONTROL YOUR EMPATH EMOTIONS?	41
STEPS TO CONTROL EMPATH FEELINGS	42
THE EMPATH RELATIONSHIP GUIDE	44
THE EMPATH RELATIONSHIP GUIDE	46
OVERCOMING SOCIAL ANXIETY FOR EMPATHS	48
THE SYMPTOMS OF SOCIAL ANXIETY IN EMPATHS	51
STEPS TO OVERCOME SOCIAL ANXIETY FOR EMPATHS	52
THOUGHT REPLACEMENT GUIDE FOR EMPATHS HAVING SOCIAL ANXIETY	54

HOW TO CREATE POSITIVE RELATIONSHIPS. HOW TO NAVIGATE INTIMATE RELATIONSHIPS WITHOUT FEELING OVERWHELMED 55

LIST OF POSITIVE PRACTICES EMPATHS CAN PRACTICE TO BE INTIMATE WITHOUT BEING OVERWHELMED.. 60

EMOTIONAL MANAGEMENT TECHNIQUES FOR EMPATHS............................. 61

THE THREE STEP EMOTION MANAGEMENT GUIDE FOR EMPATHS................................ 65
KNOW HOW YOU FEEL -- A TEST FOR LABELING EMOTIONS 66

THE EMPATH SITUATION TEST 68

HOW TO FIND THE RIGHT WORK FOR EMPATHS... 74

TOOLS FOR PROTECTING YOURSELF FROM SENSORY OVERLOAD, EXHAUSTION, ADDICTIONS, AND COMPASSION FATIGUE WHILE REPLENISHING YOUR VITAL ENERGY.. 78

MEDITATION AND BREATHING TECHNIQUES THAT ARE SPECIALLY CREATED FOR EMPATHS 84

BREATHING EXERCISES FOR EMPATHS 86
MEDITATION AND YOGA FOR EMPATHS 89
THE BALANCE OF CHAKRAS 91

LIFE HACKS FOR AN EMPATH 92

GUIDANCE FOR PARENTING AND RAISING EMPATHETIC CHILDREN 97

THE 10 WARNING SIGNS THAT TELLS YOU THAT YOUR CHILD IS AN EMPATH 99
EFFECTIVE PARENTING STRATEGIES FOR DEALING WITH EMPATHS 101

EMPATH SURVIVAL NUGGETS TO BE A SKILLED EMPATH 103

CONCLUSION.. 107

Introduction

Empaths are people who think "I don't just listen to your words, I listen to how you use them. I listen to the tone of your voice, your body movements, and subtle facial expressions. I interpret your silences, I can hear everything you don't say in words."

Instagram Me.Me

"Empaths" are people who put others before themselves, think, feel and understand others in an intense and deep-rooted way. Empaths always go extra miles to make things better for others and build a strong interpersonal connection with them.

Empaths are those who

- Use kind words
- Make people feel important and understood
- Value what others think
- Accept and appreciate individual differences
- Encourage others to develop empathy.

In this book, we are going to focus not only on empathy as a skill but on **Empaths** -- the people who go beyond being just 'empathetic.' The thin line of difference that exists between empathy and being an empath is a major focus here. It is a survival guide including life hacks to develop, survive and sustain being an empath, what challenges they face and how they can overcome the hurdles of an Empath life.

Understanding Empathy

The Difference between Empath and Empathy

"Empathy is about finding echoes of another person in yourself."

Mohsin Hamid

Have you ever tried walking in someone else's shoes?

***

It is a Sunday morning, and you are at home with no work, all in a good mood. Suddenly the doorbell rings. You open the door and find out a salesboy standing with his items. He requests you to buy his items and tries to persuade you in all possible ways, and after a certain time you lose temper and slam the door right on his face.

***

Firstly, you didn't do anything wrong. It's Sunday after all, and you had no requirement to buy the item. Now, try switching the roles for a second and imagine yourself as the salesboy who is working door-to-door on Sundays and is getting yelled at for doing nothing but his job. How do you feel?

Empathy is the ability to understand someone from their perspective. It helps us to understand others' feelings under different circumstances. The concept of Empathy was introduced by German Psychologists and has two broad explanations now.

The traditional approach of empathy says it is the emotional connection between two people.

The more contemporary approach defines empathy to be the endeavor to understand someone from their perspective.

Whether you go by the first approach or the second one, empathy is a skill that is essential for a better living. It is not only a gift for the one who gets it, but it is also a great feeling for the one who gives it too.

Who is an Empath?

Empath is one who can read and realize others' emotions and feelings without being told. The terms *empathy* and *Empath* are very close to each other but are not completely the same. An Empath is someone who has the ability to immerse himself completely into someone else's being and feel what that person feels. An empath does not require any reason or incident to trigger the feeling, they have an inbuilt urge of understanding others.

Difference between Empath and Empathy

- Empathy is usually preceded by a trigger or a physical signal (like a phone call or a meeting, etc.). But an Empath would not require any external cues to revive his sense of compassion and insight.

- We all can be empathetic, but being an Empath is a true gift - rare to find. An Empath can be the source of heal, the answer to pains and a true guiding light for the ones in need.

- The exchange of mental energy is very powerful in Empaths. Showing empathy can simply be imagining how it feels like to be in someone's position, but an Empath can literally bring himself to that place and use all his mental energy in realizing the other person. Empaths have powerful minds and strong intuitions.

QUALITIES OF AN EMPATH

"One doesn't have to operate with great malice to do great harm. The absence of Empathy and Understanding are sufficient."

Charles M. Blow

Empaths are highly sensitive people who stand out from others in terms of their sensibility, compassion, and understanding.

Empaths have some features that make them unique and special from others:

- They have heightened awareness to vague or low-intensity stimuli.
- They are highly reactive and become easily attached to others on an emotional level.
- They are the ones who suffer without complaining.
- They are emotionally labile.
- They always walk an extra mile when it comes to helping someone in need.
- They are reliable, honest and altruistic.
- They often stay behind the limelight and doesn't like being the center of attention.
- They are selfless.
- They are non-judgmental in approach.

Can you relate any of these feelings to yourself? If you are, then it is possible you are an empath too. We will find out more about it in the following sections.

ARE YOU AN EMPATH?

"Be somebody who makes everybody feel like a somebody." --
Proverb

Empathy is a skill that can be developed and learned. But whether you are an Empath or not is an underlying trait. Empaths absorb the emotions and energy of others and perceive what they feel. Being an empath is a black and white phenomenon. You are either an Empath, or you are not.

10 signs that you are an Empath

There are some attributes common in all Empaths. If you are an Empath, you will have one or more of the following traits.

1. You reach out to help others without them asking you.
2. You know how others' feel without them telling you.
3. You can feel others' pains and sorrows.
4. You can pick up others' pains -even physical ones, and make them your own.
5. You have a strong, very strong imaginative power.
6. People find you trustworthy and confide in you all the time.
7. You always go extra miles in helping people, even strangers in public places.
8. You care about animals and will always save them from any danger.
9. You are an active listener.
10. You are non-judgemental. You listen to understand, not to judge.

Types of Empath

- **Emotional Empath** - They can connect to others on an emotional level by feeling their happiness, pain, and grief. Emotional empaths are huge supports for those undergoing relationship stress, divorce, break-ups, or separation from loved ones.

- **Social Empath** - Social Empaths are those who step forward to help people irrespective of whether they know them or not. They find immense pleasure in social works, alleviation of the weak and oppressed people and even don't mind helping strangers who are in need.

- **Medical Empath** - These people have an intuitive power of connecting to the physical energies of other people. They know what is best for an ailing person and can feel the pain almost physically themselves. The energy transmission for medical or physical empaths are the highest and most intense ones.

- **Telepathic Empath** - The highest level of intuition and gut feeling rests on telepathic Empaths. They can understand what a person is going through with or without verbal communication. Telepathic empaths can comprehend the external and internal cucs in a way very few can.

- **Flora and Fauna Empath** - People who are plant or animal empaths sense the needs of plants and animals and grow a strong connection with them. They know the right place and the right way to nurture them, and they can telepathically interact with them.

If you are an empath, it doesn't imply you will have all these traits. You may have a combination or may be just an Empath in a single category.

THE SELF-HELP TEST FOR EMPATHS

Below is a list of 10 statements about yourself. Rate the statements on a 5 point scale where 0 would mean "strongly disagree," and 5 would mean "strongly agree." The sum up of the scores would suggest whether you are an Empath or not.

Statement	Rating 0 - Strongly Disagree 5- Strongly Agree					
1. I can feel others' pains.	0	1	2	3	4	**(5)**
2. I know what a person is going through even without talking to him.	0	1	2	3	4	**(5)**
3. I feel emotionally drained from hearing about other people's sorrows.	0	1	2	3	4	**(5)**
4. I never think twice before helping others.	0	1	2	3	4	**(5)**
5. I love growing plants and nurturing them.	0	1	**(2)**	3	4	5
6. I feel an uncontrollable urge to help whenever I see someone in need.	0	1	2	**(3)**	4	5
7. I enjoy social work.	0	1	2	**(3)**	4	5
8. I cannot see animals in pain. It breaks my heart.	0	1	2	3	4	**(5)**
9. I am aware of my strengths and weaknesses	0	1	2	3	**(4)**	5
10. I can never label a person as good or bad without knowing what he is going through.	0	1	2	**(3)**	4	5

Total Score (out of 50)	36

Sum up the ratings for each statement. The higher your score out of 50, the higher would be the chances that you are an Empath.

My total score is -

36

A score of 25 and above would mean you possess majority of the qualities of an Empath and a score below 15 would mean you do not possess the qualities of an empath.

EMPATHY SPECTRUM

"The opposite of anger is not calmness, it is Empathy." --
Mehmet Oz

The explanation of the Empathy Spectrum has been a fascinating move in understanding human behavior. Understanding human behavior is the most complex task and can be extremely exhausting. There is no single theory that can fully explain all attributes of human behavior.

The writings of <u>Baron- Cohen</u> in "**The Science of Empathy**" has thrown some light to the **Theory of Empathy Spectrum**. They have stated that all humans lie along a spectrum or continuum of Empathy, some towards the higher end and some towards the lower end.

Think of it this way. When a child trips off in the classroom, many of his classmates will laugh, while some would come forward to offer his help. Why this difference? What makes two people who share same cultural, social, and intellectual attributes act so differently?

The Empathy Spectrum Curve

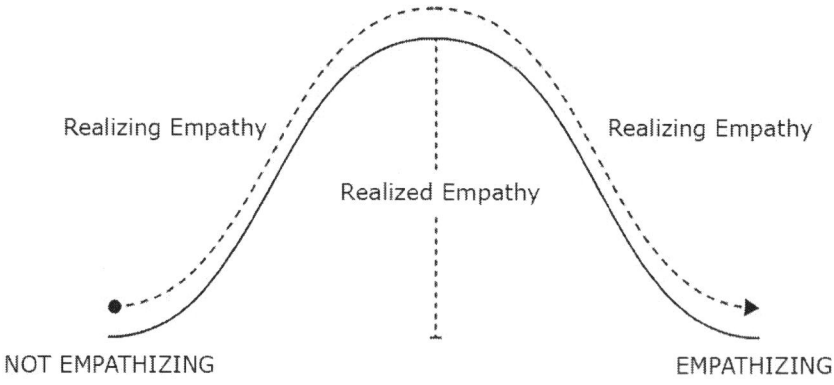

The difference in empathy is seen in people across the spectrum. Those who are empaths, have an empathy level above average and lie towards the positive end of the spectrum while those who have empathy levels below average lie towards the negative end of the spectrum.

There are ranges of empathy levels across the spectrum and different subtypes as mentioned in the previous chapter.

A recent study on Empathy Spectrum has come up with the role of "*mirror neurons*" in explaining empathic behaviors. According to the study, we all have some "mirror neurons" in our brains that activate with visual and auditory cues. For example, when you see a person crying in front of you, you may suddenly have a flashback to a time when you cried in a similar way. This recollection or reciprocation of feelings is the role of "mirror neurons."

Empaths have a higher activation of these neurons as a result of which they are more reactive and emotionally aroused than others who have lesser reactive mirror neuron functions.

A complete 'zero' empathy is rarely seen. Usually, empaths are clustered at one extreme of the Empathy Spectrum, and the Apathetic ones lie at the opposite extremity.

For example, individuals with Autism Spectrum Disorders usually have a low score on empathy, and they clutter towards the negative side of the scale. The theory of Empathy Spectrum believes that it is hard to manage feelings of empathy for those who have a very high score. For example, scientists believe that individuals with specific mental disabilities like Asperger's Syndrome are so intense in their feelings of empathy that it becomes difficult for them to focus and they end up exhibiting unwanted mannerisms.

SCIENTIFIC THEORIES RELATED TO EMPATH AND EMPATHY

"The path to gaining respect is paved with knowledge and empathy." -- Evan Brown.

The Theory of Electromagnetic fields –

This scientific theory backs the emotional hypersensitivity of Empaths. It states that we all have an electromagnetic field that emits information and vibes about us. Empaths are highly sensitive and susceptible to these inputs and become overwhelmed by external stimulation.

The Dopamine Hypothesis Theory –

An important finding in the physiology and brain function of empaths is the Dopamine Hypothesis Theory. Dopamine is a neurotransmitter that is essential for our emotional responses and affectability. Increased dopamine activity has been associated with pleasure responses. The dopamine hypothesis states that introvert empaths have lesser dopamine activity than extroverted empaths, which is why the former find pleasure with less stimulating activities like reading, spending time alone, while the latter always need more stimuli to trigger their emotions.

Hoffman's Empathy Theory –

The Hoffman's Theory of Empathy is one of the most important theoretical base for empaths. Martin Hoffman, in his theory of moral psychology, has focused on empathy and empaths. The concept of empathic distress was a major focus of Hoffman's Theory. He explained that empaths undergo distress that is associated with helping others and is reduced after the help is done. The theory further categorizes the development of empath distress into five categories through the developmental stages.

The newborn reactive cry
The first stage where there is only distress with no effort to reduce it. It is the first empath reaction of an infant.

Egocentric distress
This comes during the end of first year and second year, where the child recognizes the pain of another infant. However, the child aims to reduce his distress rather than helping the other one. Hence the term "egocentric distress."

Quasi-egocentric distress

In the next year the quasi-egocentric distress develops where the child aims to help others to reduce distress, but from his/her own perspective. Ability to see from a different perspective is still absent.

Veridical distress

From this stage, the child starts developing the actual abilities of an empath. It continues to grow throughout life and gets mature with each year. The child learns to look into matters with others' perspectives and steps out to help others to reduce their empathy distress.

Distress beyond the situation

Empathy beyond the situation is a stage where the empaths are no longer happy with just helping others. They literally involve themselves in others' lives and are remarkably affected by what others are going through -- even the small things or the ones that are beyond control.

Simulation Theory of Empathy

Simulation Theory is the most popular theory backing empathy and empaths. Based on the philosophies of Alvin Goldman and Robert Gordon, this theory stresses the role of mirror neurons in development of empathic feelings. Mirror neurons are special brain cells that are responsible for feelings of pain, altruism, and satisfaction -- the key emotions guiding an empath. The reason why an empath feels sad in others' pains, worries for others or gets pleasure in doing things better for people around them are all due to the actions of the mirror neurons. The more activity in the mirror neurons, the stronger would be the empathy feelings.

Living life as an Empath

Nuggets to embrace your Empath

gift

"The great gift of human beings is that we have the power of Empathy." -- Meryl Streep.

How does being an Empath feels

****

Since his early years, Sam had been a sensitive kid. He had a hard time concentrating on his work. He kept wondering what others around him were thinking. He tried to read their faces and thought he could understand how they feel. He felt tired and exhausted every day after he came home.

****

Can you imagine how it would feel to be exhausted and drained out all the time?

Empaths have a constant feeling of apprehension and concern. They are worried about how people around them are thinking, feeling and undergoing. They often end up feeling emotionally drained and exhausted after being around people. Empaths are so involved centering their thoughts around other people that they fail to achieve things for themselves. Living as an Empath is actively feeling others all the time. An empath never has to make an effort or wait for anyone to ask before being understood. But it is not always the easy way.

Tips to embrace your Empath gift

People are not born with empathy. It can be grown and cultivated throughout life. Here is a list of some easy and simple steps that you can follow to embrace and accept the gift of empathy.

Judge less.
Empaths have the special ability to walk in others' shoes. No matter who they are or how unacceptable they might be to the world, if you are an empath, you will be able to see the world from their perspective.

Control your emotions.
It is expected that if you are an empath, you will be easily moved and get overwhelmed by what others are feeling. Restrain yourself from getting carried away and make your empath qualities mean something to someone.

Develop a strong connection with yourself.
Empaths have the unique ability to immerse completely into being someone else. But at the same time, connection with the self is also indispensable.

Vent out the blues.
Try using any stress relieving techniques that work for you. It is important not to lose inner peace after all.

Take responsibilities, but wisely.
Do not blame yourself for what is beyond your control.

Do not let negativity overpower your positive wave.
Empaths can absorb energy from people around them which is why you should remember not to internalize any negative fervor.

Don't be a mousetrap to woes.
Empaths have the virtue of making people confide in them. Any person can just come and start venting out their feelings to you leaving you overwrought and grieved. Set reasonable boundaries and do not allow everything affect you.

Growing as an Empath

Empathy begins at home. Expressing empathy at home with each member of the family, including outgroup family members like drivers, servants, housekeepers, etc., helps to build strong relationships and mutual support.

Examples of how you can embrace your empath gift

- o You hear your dad talking about the bad day he had. You can show empathy by listening to him talking about the troubles. Try to understand why he is upset.

- o Your younger brother is upset as he has broken his favorite toy. It may have been his fault, but if you are an empath, you will understand how he is feeling right now. Sit beside him, wipe his tears and express your empathy by telling him about a time you had felt the same way.

- o Learning to be an empath in school helps you to be a good friend. We can show empathy in school by showing our classmates we care, understand them, and see things from their point of view.

- Your classmate raised her hand but gave an incorrect answer. The whole class starts laughing at her silliness. Show empathy to your friend by not laughing at her. Tell her something sweet and tell her that you understand how humiliated she felt.

- Your friend is fat and gets bullied every day at school. Express your empath ability by supporting him. Let him know he is just as good as others and never laugh at him.

- Show empathy in the community by helping others. Widen your perspective, learn about how people vary in their thinking, you could donate, work for public interest and help those who are in need. A community is a group of people who live and work together. They share same thoughts, ideologies, philosophies and religious views too. Developing empathy in the community is mostly about being open-minded and embracing diversities.

CONTROL YOUR EMPATH ABILITIES

"The deepest pain I ever felt was denying my own feelings to make everyone else comfortable" --Nicole Lyons

Controlling Empath abilities - Why is it important to control your Empath emotions?

Empaths learn and develop their abilities by accepting others and appreciating the differences. But at the same time, you must also remember where to restrain your feelings. If you allow your emotions to flow, you will end up feeling mentally exhausted and grieved. Break the connection once a while to restore your inner happiness.

Why is it important to control your Empath feelings

Controlling empath feelings is important for the following reasons.

- o To avoid being overwhelmed
- o To avoid mental distress
- o To ensure mental and physical well-being
- o To maintain focus on yourself
- o To avoid being unduly exploited

Steps to control Empath feelings

It may sound easy, but controlling emotions can be a really difficult task to do -- especially for the HSPs (Highly Sensitive Persons). Here are a few tricks that you can follow to manage your emotions effectively so that they do not become a twinge. Empaths consider it as a bliss if they can regulate their feelings and control how they feel. Now let's get to the hope.

1. Isolate yourself from others for at least 10 minutes every day. It helps to declutter the mind.

2. Follow your intuitions. If you feel you are absorbing too much negative energy from someone around, distance yourself from him/her.

3. Do not overthink. Overthinking increases the emotional load.

4. Trust facts more than words.

5. Spend more time with people who make you happy.

6. Do not presume or read minds. As an Empath, you may have intuitive thoughts about how others feel. But try not to be overwhelmed before someone actually confides.

7. Concentrate on the practical issues like job, studies, etc.. Do not let emotions sabotage your well-being.

THE EMPATH RELATIONSHIP GUIDE

"Be a rainbow in someone else's cloud" -- *Maya Angelou.*

Managing life successfully is sometimes a challenge for the Empaths. Out of the many important areas of life, relationship is something that requires extra effort to keep it going. And by relationship here I am referring to any informal bonding of love - that may or may not be just the romantic partner. Not only for empaths, people around them, who love them, also face some critical issue that may be rough for the relationship. It is not that there are only disadvantages of being around an Empath, there are definite bright sides of it too.

So for those of the HSPs who crave for a successful relationship but fail to achieve it, here is how you can start working on it.

The Empath Relationship guide

***

You may feel that your partner doesn't understand you or is too selfish or insensitive. You may be so engrossed in doing good for others that you end up neglecting the closest person you have.

***

These are some of the common feelings that Empaths have in their relationships, and they often fail to hold the happiness in it.

1. **Time** - Devote as much time as you can to your partner. Never let him/her feel less important.

2. **Caging** - Do not let yourself be trapped in the woes and worries of others such that you fail to notice the reasons to be happy. Free yourself and experience your life.

3. **Acceptance** - Once you accept that you are unique and your partner is not as sensitive as you, things won't be that difficult anymore.

4. **Understanding** - Develop a strong and mutually supportive relationship where you both complement each other.

5. **Miscommunications** - Never leave any space for miscommunication with your loved ones. Tell them how you feel, share your emotional burden. Not only would it relax you, but it will also make the partner feel he/she is important.

OVERCOMING SOCIAL ANXIETY FOR EMPATHS

"In a world full of people who couldn't care less, be someone who couldn't care more."

Proverb

You go in a social gathering with your friends and family around. All decked up and happy, you go in with a happy heart and want to participate fully. But instead, you start feeling anxious. You feel your heart pounding, hands sweating and voice trembling. Does this situation sound familiar?

Empaths often suffer from social anxiety that affects their interpersonal communication and relationships. Being around people make empaths conscious, and they start apprehending what is going on in the minds of people around them.

Studies conducted on empathy and mental health have shown that people who have high empathy scores are the ones showing symptoms of social anxiety. They become overwhelmed by reactions of people around them and develop anxiety over it. The hypersensitivity of empaths makes them sense the positive or negative energy that is around them, and they catch it up. As a result, empaths often tend to avoid social situations and feel extreme discomfort when facing people.

Overcoming social anxiety for empaths is a very vital issue for their well-being and happiness. But before discussing the steps of overcoming social anxiety, it is important to know when to worry. Social Anxiety comes with a bunch of warning signals. Be aware. If you experience them, know that it is time you start managing your anxious self.

The symptoms of Social Anxiety in Empaths

Physical Symptoms

- Palpitations
- Increased blood pressure and pulse rate
- Sweating
- Blushing and heat flushes
- Dizziness
- Muscular numbness and feeling giddy

Psychological and behavioral symptoms

- Excessive worry over what others are thinking
- Fear of being judged, criticized, or rejected
- Avoiding the feared situation
- Isolation from group

Steps to overcome social anxiety for Empaths

- **Identify** the negative thoughts that accompany you when you are in social situations.

- **Focus on "the moment"** and what is going on now. Forget all anticipations and mind readings.

- **Breathe slowly.** Our breathing tends to get faster when we experience anxiety. Try to stay calm and regulate your breaths when you feel your nerves getting of control.

- Try to **challenge your negative thoughts** and replace them with positive thoughts like "I can do it," "I look beautiful," "I will concentrate on my work and nothing else," "Nobody will laugh at me," etc.

- **Expose yourself to the feared situations**. Attend social gatherings, meetings, hangouts, initiate conversations and speak out about yourself.

- **Practice relaxation techniques** like Yoga, Meditation, and Mindfulness.

- If you feel your anxiety going beyond your control, **try talking to a therapist**. Cognitive Behavioral Therapy is one of the best-known solutions for Social Anxiety.

Thought Replacement Guide for Empaths having Social Anxiety

Situation	Negative Thought provoking Anxiety	Alternate Positive Thoughts
You are eating out with a group of people you don't know much.	1. I can't cope. 2. I am looking stupid. 3. My hands are trembling. I will spill the coffee. 4. I don't fit here. 5. If I talk, they will understand how nervous I am.	1. I can cope. 2. I look beautiful. 3. I have been in similar situations before. I can handle this. 4. I fit here. It is just going to be okay. 5. All are friends. No one will judge me.

How to Create Positive Relationships.

How to Navigate Intimate Relationships without Feeling Overwhelmed

---

"I believe Empathy is the most essential quality of civilization."

Roger Ebert

The emotional connection is so strong in empaths that they feel overwhelmed and emotionally burdened sometimes. It is essential that empaths get some time alone to declutter their minds and re-focus on their relationships. Positive Psychology or the science of happiness believes that happiness can be found in life when

1. We look at life with optimism.

2. Appreciate the present.

3. Accept and make peace with the past.

4. Be grateful and forgive others.

5. Look beyond the momentary pleasures and pains.

Empaths may sometimes unknowingly sabotage their relationships. Their sense of generosity, help, care, and sacrifice becomes so big that it overpowers their relationships, thus causing relationship clutters. It is not rare to find empaths who are loners, and one of the major reason is perhaps they couldn't make their relationships work out.

Normal relationship troubles and the relationship issues with an empath are not the same. And not an easy job for either of the partners. There has to be a well-defined boundary along with an intimate bond of love and trust that can make a relationship work successfully with an Empath.

Some strategies for Empaths for building a positive and long lasting relationship

1. **Give love, to yourself and others** - Love yourself before you can gift your love to anyone else. Being an empath, one may often forget to show love to oneself. Remember "you" matter. Exchange love but also give it to yourself first.
2. **Conserve and protect your energy** - Empaths fail to limit their care and service for others. Even if it is for the wrong person. See who you are spending your energy on. Embrace people with positive vibes.

3. **Laugh your heart out** - Never be so engrossed in others' sorrows that you forget to share your own happiness. No matter what, spending some joyful moments with your partner can work wonders in building a long-lasting bond.

4. **Share** - You might feel you are the one who should absorb the pains and problems of others and keep enduring your own. Never do that. If you are in a relationship, allow your partner to be "your" empath and share your feelings. There is no harm in letting your guards down once in a while. Just like you

share others' problems, share yours too. That would make your partner feel important and loved.

5. **Embrace differences -** It would be absurd to expect that empaths would have a relationship with other empaths. Nothing comes that easy. If you are an empath and your partner is not, do not let it jeopardize your relation. Accept the individual differences and build mutual respect for each other. That would help in making the relationship deep and mature.

List of positive practices empaths can practice to be intimate without being overwhelmed

- o Do not judge your partner based on what he/she tells.

- o Do not try to presume what is not told.

- o Try to stay focused in the moment.

- o Engage in healthy and positive communications.

- o Take some time out for yourself as often you want.

- o Never hide your feelings. If you are happy, express it, if you are sad, share it.

- o Trust your partner and make him/her feel important.

- o Keep your priorities clear to each other.

Communicate as often as possible. Try to meet and talk face to face rather than through calls or texts.

Emotional management techniques for Empaths

"Empathy is seeing with the eyes of another, listening with the ears of another and feeling with the heart of another"

Proverb

One big problem with being an empath is we start feeling for the wrong people too. There is huge emotional investment behind those who don't deserve it. The overstimulation and hypersensitivity makes an empath emotionally imbalanced. As a result, problems in other important areas like profession, family, and health starts showing up.

Before talking about the emotional regulation strategies, let us talk a little about what do we mean by regulating emotions. Emotional regulation is the employment of tactics that would influence our emotions positively. We subconsciously do this all the time. For example, going for a walk, eating chocolates, hanging out with friends may lift up your mood when you are sad. We just need to be adept in implementing the right techniques.

Emotional regulation, or maintaining a balance in the way empaths feel is very important for their healthy functioning. Here are few simple strategies that could help an empath find an emotional balance.

- **Observe** before you react. Pay attention to what is going on around you and think before you get flowed into emotions.

- **Feel** yourself. Empaths are often so emotionally charged that they misinterpret the experience. Be absolutely sure of the exact emotion - whether it is anger or jealousy, sadness or disappointment, happiness or ecstasy. Once you are able to label how you feel, regulating emotions would not be a difficult task anymore.

- **Let go** of what you cannot control. Being an empath, we may have this uncontrollable urge of fixing everything up; but there are certain things that are beyond control. No matter how hard you try, you cannot save everyone from pain.

- **Be Mindful.** Focus on the present. Use all your five senses to feel what is going on around you right now. Use mindfulness as a break from the daily stresses and remove the mental blocks that hold you down. You can try mindful meditation, mindful breathing, mindful listening or mindful observing.

- **Cling to positive experiences.** If you are struggling with your emotions and failing to handle them right, it is time you embrace more positive experiences. Positivity is a healing in itself. Choose anything that works for you -- it may be a nature walk, talking to a friend, playing with a kid, watching cartoons, donating, do more things that make you feel good.

- **Vent out** your emotions. Bottling up how you feel does no good. Share your feelings to lessen the burden. Write them, say them aloud, or talk about them to somebody - cry when you are sad, laugh when you are happy, show it when you are angry. The more you express emotions, in the right way, the less you would have trouble managing them.

- **Ask for help.** Empaths seldom do so. But it is always a good idea to reach out for professional help when your emotional regulation strategies are not enough to hold you together. Talk to a counselor or a therapist if you need. It would not do any worse.

- **Have a journal** where you can write down about how you feel. Empaths often hesitate to share what they feel because people around them don't think the same way. Be your own friend. Have an emotion journal and open up all your feelings into it. It is one of the most effective emotional regulation skills one can practice.

The Three Step Emotion Management Guide for Empaths

Step 1 - Understand	**Step 2 - Control**	**Step 3 - Maintain**
1. Identify your emotions. 2. Know what triggers them. 3. Notice how you feel. 4. Label your emotions correctly.	1. Choose your reactions wisely. 2. Do not get overflowed in emotions. 3. Allow yourself to breathe and let go. 4. Accept your limitations. 5. Employ strategies that are suitable for you.	1. Act consistently. 2. Practice the emotional regulation techniques you have chosen to follow. 3. Do not feel bad all the time. Let happiness find its way to your life.

Know how you feel -- A test for labeling emotions

The first step to emotional regulation is knowing how you feel and when you feel so. List down 3 situations where you felt a strong emotion.

Please, write:

Name

> CLARE

I felt happy when

1. Elexey is happy
2. I'm at Disney world
3. Knowing my Great is still with me in spirit
4. Being around my friends.
5. I'm encouraged to be me.

I felt sad when

1. I think about Elexey being sad/upset
2. Great passed away
3. I can't help my family with their problems
4. Lack of communication between people
5. I feel others' pain/upset

I felt angry when
1. Grant was treated badly / passed away
2. Dad speaks to me aggressively.
3. I'm given no choice over matters that concern me.
4. People are insensitive towards others feelings.
5. family members not addressing their issues / problems.

THE EMPATH SITUATION TEST

"One of the best ways to show empathy is by encouraging others to do so"

Shannon Welbourn

Empaths react differently than other people. They are more sensitive, emotional and catchy when it comes to any social situation. The Empath Situation Test is an easy and fun way to gain insight into yourself. It lets you externalize your behavior and improve the ways you can react in a situation.

There are four situations given. Read each situation and suggest how you would have felt or reacted to it. This is a qualitative test hence no right or wrong. Be your own judge.

Take a pen and paper and list down the possible ways you would react to these different circumstances. The purpose of this test is to increase your self-awareness. Once you have listed your reactions, try to think how else you can react to decrease the emotional burden?

Situation 1: Your driver comes late to pick you up from school. He apologizes for the delay, but your mom talks rudely to him for making you wait after school.

- ☐ How would you feel?

Embarrassed. Sorry for the driver.

- ☐ What would you do/say him?

Tell him I understand and not to worry about it.

- ☐ What do you think should be the right way to react in such a situation?

Not to be embarrassed by someone else's behaviour.

Situation 2: Your brother, who studied really hard for an exam scored unexpectedly poor in it. Parents and teachers are scolding him for being so careless in studies.

☐ How would you feel?

Sad that he is being scolded.

☐ What would you tell your brother?

That he did his best and exam scores aren't really that important in the whole scheme of things.

Situation 3: A new girl joins your class who is from a different country and speaks a different language. She stands out among your other classmates, and people make fun of how she looks.

☐ How would you feel?

upset for her.

☐ What would you tell her?

Not to listen to the others — she is perfect as she is.

☐ What, according to you should be the correct way of behaving in such a situation?

Become her friend + encourage her to be herself.

Situation 4: Your team has won the inter-state cricket championship. You stand cheering with your team while you suddenly observe the other team players standing quietly nearby.

☐ How would you feel?

happy for my team. But understand the others disappointment.

☐ What would you tell them?

well done - they did their best.

How to Find the Right Work for Empaths

"How you make others feel about themselves, says a lot about you."

Proverb

Much of empath distress comes from work stress and hazards. They find difficult to fit in the competitive environment and become easily affected. Jobs including regular customer transactions brings extreme distress to empaths as they start focusing on people they deal with rather than the work they are doing.

Considering this, choosing the right career path for the empath is very vital. Normally, empaths are expected to flourish in low-stress jobs or service-oriented works like teaching or medicine. Creativity attracts empaths, and they also prefer being self-employed. Empaths are often called "**energy vampires**" because of their unique ability of attracting energy from people around them.

Professions best-suited for empaths

Empaths perform great in professions that involve creativity and providing service. Works that can reflect the qualities of an empath in the real world are the ones best-suited for highly sensitive people. Helping professions, creative jobs, and self-employed business are preferred by the HSPs (highly sensitive person). They must make the most of their sensitivity to succeed in their workplace. It is easy for them to get swayed by the emotions of people around them --

including clients, patients, or colleagues, which is why low-stress jobs are more suitable for them.

- Healthcare professions like doctors, nurses, naturopaths, etc.
- Creative jobs like painting, writing, etc.
- Teaching
- Social and Public services
- Animal-related careers like animal sitters, pet specialists, etc.
- Working for non-profit organizations
- Counselling and mental health jobs like psychologists, counselors, therapists, rehabilitators, etc.

Jobs to avoid

Empaths, as we already discussed before, are blessed with the dexterity of consuming energy from people around them - positive and negative. High-stress jobs like sales and marketing are perceived as too draining and emotionally destroying by empaths. Especially for empaths who are also introverts, customer dealings are extremely painful and mentally tiresome. Sensitive people who work in sales jobs often report to be feeling weary, and it is extremely difficult for them to deal with people the whole day. Researches on the mental health and well-being of empaths have clearly suggested the kind of jobs that are least suitable for them. These jobs include

- o Sales, marketing and retail jobs like working in a store, or selling and gaining profits for the company
- o Political jobs
- o Public relation jobs like manager, recruiter, etc.

Being around people and dealing with them makes an empath overwhelmed. They lose focus on the job and invest all their energy in other people. The best jobs for empaths are therefore the ones where they can get to invest more energy in themselves and work without being overwhelmed.

Tools for Protecting Yourself from Sensory Overload, Exhaustion, Addictions, and Compassion Fatigue While Replenishing Your Vital Energy

"Empathy is a quality of character that can change the world."

Barrack Obama

One big obstacle for empaths is that they absorb negative energy from others. Have you ever felt you can sense what someone is trying to convey through his/her mannerisms? Empaths often report that they can touch, feel, hear, see and smell what others cannot. As a result, their comprehension of others' feelings goes way beyond what an average person would feel.

As a mental health professional, I had spent some time working in de-addiction centers a few years back. And to my surprise, I found there were a handful of them who were highly sensitive! Yes, you heard me right.

Out of the several effects of the emotional burden that empaths carry along with them, addiction is one. Empaths who cannot deal with the deadweight of people and their feelings and fails to find the equilibrium, resort to substances like cigarettes or alcohol to mask the pain.

***

Jane was a freshman who said she could relate to what others around her are feeling. She kept donating from her pocket money to the poor and could not bear the pain of others. She said her friends would laugh at how stupid her reactions were whenever she saw somebody getting teased or failing. Jane reported that it was unbearable for her to see others in pain and she felt helpless for them. She started bottling herself up and soon after the first year, became a heavy smoker. "I smoke to get relief, it is as if I am sharing what I am feeling."

***

So if you are an empath and your emotional drain out is blocking you from reaching where you want to be, here are some tools that can help you in shielding yourself from the emotional depletion.

- o **Stay healthy**. Do not consider your well-being to be less important. Maintain a healthy diet, choose suitable exercise and workout schedules and pay more importance to yourself.

- o **Choose to be rational**. Emotional sailing is easy for empaths. But you must try to think rationally before any actions. You must remember there are certain problems you cannot solve; certain circumstances are beyond your control, and your help might not be as welcome as you expect.

- o **Channel your empathy feelings in the most intelligent way**. Personally interfering in the matters of others might not be welcome. People often misjudge empaths for this reason. Know where you can act and hold yourself in places where you can't. Engage in self-absorbing activities like painting, singing, sports, etc., and stop yourself from overthinking.

- **Trust, but wisely**. Do not be a victim of exploitation. Being an energy vampire, empaths often fall prey to attracting negative energy. People unfairly use them to fulfill their selfish aims. Use your intuition - you are blessed with it.

- **Practice stress relief activities**. Mindfulness, meditation, Yoga, and breathing exercises are helpful in this regard. It helps to reduce the emotional burden and reach a state of relaxation. It is essential for physical and mental well-being. Try using fidget spinners, stress balls and stress cubes as tools for stress reduction.

- **Use your senses fully**. Our sense organs are extremely powerful and using them in the right way can protect empaths to shield themselves from the weariness. Use the seeing, listening, smelling, touching and tasting senses optimally to achieve wellness. Follow the sense-by-sense guide shown below.

1. **See**
   - Visualize soothing and happy images in mind when you are alone.
   - Watch your favorite movie or cartoon.
   - Admire the nature and its beauty.
2. **smell**
   - Experience fragrances, natural or artificial perfumes and see how it calms your mind.
3. **hear**
   - Listen to music as often and for as long as you want. Choose your favorite tracks, or soft melodious tunes and spend time alone refreshing your mind while listening to them.
4. **taste**
   - Go out and grab your favorite delicacies. Pamper yourself with the food you love to eat. Have icecreams, go to your favorite coffee bar and indulge yourself. It brings down the woes and lightens up your mood immediately.
5. **touch**
   - Cuddle with your pet.
   - Be intimate with your partner and spend time close together.

   - **Seek professional help** to get yourself out of any substance abuse. It might be difficult to initiate the process, but do not step back from taking any step that promotes your well-being. Keep yourself as a priority.

MEDITATION AND BREATHING TECHNIQUES THAT ARE SPECIALLY CREATED FOR EMPATHS

"As one goes through life one learns if you don't paddle your own canoe, you don't move."

Katherine Hepburn.

It is a challenge for empaths to be grounded and settled with an ongoing mental turbulence all the time. The psychic energy and telepathic exchanges make them mentally tired and often depressed.

Mediation and yoga have always been the best solution when it comes to regaining inner peace, and for empaths, the need is indispensable. There are special Yoga, breathing, meditation, and relaxation techniques that are designed for empaths. Let's have a look at them.

Breathing exercises for Empaths

Air is the life force that guides our survival. Controlling and regulating breaths not only relieves stress but also increases metabolism rate and helps to maintain equilibrium.

***Nadi Shodhana* or Alternate Nostril Breathing** - This is a *Pranayama* technique specially designed for empaths to help them retrieve their mental energy and preventing mental or physical breakdown. Practicing this once or twice daily has been proved to reduce the emotional burden and induce a state of relief to the empaths.

- Step 1 - Sit in a comfortable position with your back straight.
- Step 2 - Close your eyes and take two deep breaths at first.
- Step 3 - Cover your right nostril with the tip of your right thumb and inhale through the left nostril till the count of 3. Put the ring finger above the left nostril but do not touch it.
- Step 4 - Cover the left nostril and exhale through the right nostril on a count of 5. While you exhale through the right nostril, make sure your thumb is over the nostril, but not touching it.

- Step 5 - Repeat the process not less than 10 times. You may feel dizzy at the beginning, do not worry as it is the body's way of signaling that you are resting down.

Conscious Breathing for Empaths - Breathing affects our thoughts, emotions, and behavior. It has healing power for empaths as focused breathing clears the state of confusion and helps in reaching clarity. Conscious breathing can be practiced through *Pranayama, Yoga, or Meditation.* The key concept in conscious breathing is to be mindful and notice the upward and downward flow of the muscles while you breathe. It is highly recommended for Empaths and HSPs because they often forget their own contentment while healing the woes and wounds of others.

- Step 1 - Choose a peaceful place where you can practice. Sit with your back straight and choose a comfortable posture. You can tune in to some soft music in low volume to induce a soothing environment or use dim lights to make yourself more comfortable.
- Step 2 - Close your eyes and try to indulge into thinking something that makes you feel good.

- Step 3 - Slowly start breathing in and out. Take deep breaths. Inhale with a count of 5 and exhale on a count of 7.
- Step 4 - Notice how your chest and your stomach falls and rises with each breath you take. Try to calm all your nerves down and focus just on your breaths.
- Step 5 - Repeat the process for no less than 20 times and observe the changes in your mind and body after the exercise is over.

Meditation and Yoga for Empaths

Yoga and Meditation are the "*Adi*" or the most primitive healing methods that were used. Not only mental and physical, but they also ensure spiritual well-being and promotes self-enhancement. The energy drain-out that empaths undergo make them vulnerable and susceptible to health hazards and other challenges. While there are different forms of physical exercises that help empath wellness, these are unarguably the best ones.

Mindful Meditation

- Step 1 - Close your eyes and find a comfortable posture -- sitting preferably.
- Step 2 – Visualize things about yourself - the things you like about yourself, a song that you like, a place you would love to go, any positive thing you associate with yourself. Let your mind wander in the positivities for a few minutes. You will find your mind jumping onto thoughts about others; consciously bring your focus back to yourself.
- Step 3 - Take deep breaths and allow yourself to float in the good thoughts. Summon your spiritual guide, a holy spirit, or a religious

messenger and devote all your thoughts unto Him.
- Step 4 - Remain in this state for few minutes, at first it would be hard to bring attention to one thing, but keep trying to concentrate. Shut the doors for empathy for a while, and release yourself from the emotional stacks. When you finish meditating, you will feel lighter and in a state of harmony.

The Balance of Chakras

In Buddhism, the concept of the *7 life chakras (wheels)* is significant for mental well-being in empaths. They believe that we have 7 chakras running through our entire body length, from root chakra (lowest chakra) to the crown chakra (topmost chakra). These chakras are responsible for regulating the hormone secretion in the bodies. The reason why empaths experience emotional burden is due to the imbalance in the chakras. Hence for empaths, maintaining an evenness in the 7 chakras is essential, and this can be achieved by

1. **Yoga** -- Yoga is often regarded as the elixir of youth and happiness for empaths. Practicing yoga improves their body functioning and allows the negative energy to gracefully find its way out of the soul.

2. **Meditation** -- Turn your back to empathy and embrace inner peace by meditating regularly. Watch videos, join meditation groups and classes, or simply practice at home using mindfulness as explained above. In any form, meditation provides instant relief and removes the affective load.

LIFE HACKS FOR AN EMPATH

"It is both a blessing and a curse to feel everything, so very deeply."

Proverb

Being grounded is a difficult task for empaths. The absorption of energy makes them engrossed in what is going on in others' lives and how they can contribute to making things better for them. However, in the process, they often end up draining all their mental energy and fall prey to distress. In this section, we will discuss some strategies, some life hacks that can be practiced by empaths regularly. These hacks work in real life and don't allow them to be energy vampires all the time.

Watch out for negative energy

If you are an empath, you cannot stop yourself from absorbing energy from being around people. Good or bad, you will consume the vibes and interpret them in a way that no one else can. Receiving massive negative energy from people around can make you physically and mentally weak. <u>Identify</u> what energizes you and what drains you out. For example, being around a baby might boost your energy. Do that more. Engage yourself with people who contribute to your well-being. In short, eliminate the bad distractions and embrace the good ones.

Change your focus

Empaths are worst at taking care of themselves. I

had a friend who was also an empath. And I hardly remember anything that he did for himself. No matter how compromising it may be, if you are an empath, you will be bent in helping others and overlooking your happiness. And this, in turn, becomes the reason you fall sick and cannot bear the pressure anymore. <u>Look at yourself as well. Focus on what makes you happy</u>. Making yourself happy is revitalizing. If you are not happy inside, you can never make people around you happy.

Follow a routine

This is an offshoot of self-help.

- Maintain a healthy diet with all the essential nutrients. A healthy diet helps the body to sustain its equilibrium or homeostasis. It is especially useful for empaths as the energy and emotional drain-out damages the brain cells and dysregulates hormonal balance.

- Stay hydrated and get enough sleep every day.

- Include a suitable workout schedule that suits your lifestyle. Yoga, meditation, gym, swimming, walking, sports, choose any or a combination of any of them. Sweating out is a great way of releasing stress and gaining clarity.

Emotional Catharsis

Vent out your emotions as often as you can. An empath's life is full of emotional loads, and unless you can find a way to ventilate, it keeps piling up to a point you can no longer handle. Use any means of catharting

- Talk to a friend

- Write down your feelings in a notebook

- Cry if you want to

- Talk to a therapist

- Express your feelings directly to the person concerned.

Establish a good relationship with yourself

As an empath, it is vital that you keep touch with yourself. Coping with the emotional overload requires that you regain the focus on yourself. Often, empaths become so devoted in consuming energy that they fail to perceive what signals their own mind and body is sending.

- o Forgive yourself and others as much possible. Not for them, but for restoring your peace. Guilt or anguish is poison for happiness.

- o Take out some "me-time" as often as you can. Spending quality time with yourself refreshes the mind and lightens the emotional load you are always carrying with you.

- o Accept your limitations. There are going to be some things you cannot control and some people you cannot help. Do not blame yourself under any circumstances.

- o Remind yourself of the blessings you have.

- o Take out time for your loved ones. Let them feel loved.

- o Choose to be happy. As an empath, you may feel appealed to all the energies hovering around you. But choose wisely before you allow any of them to impact you.

Guidance for parenting and raising empathetic children

"Empathy is when we understand before we judge."
Proverb

Raising an empath can be a real challenge. It pulls you down when you see your children suffer and you can do nothing about it. In this section, let us address the pros and cons, the effective parenting strategies, and other issue related to raising an empath.

For parents who are empaths as well, the job is easier. They can relate to their child's feelings of insecurity, emotional blunders and can be the biggest support the child can have. However, the task is more challenging for empaths having non-empath parents.

How to know if your child is an Empath?

The first step to successfully raising an empath is knowing and accepting that he/she is so. Often parents are unaware of the empath signals, and unknowingly they overlook the emotional turmoil their children are going through.

The 10 warning signs that tells you that your child is an empath

Parents must be cautious of the 10 warning signs. If your child shows one or more of them, be assured that he/she is an empath.

1. The child feels too deeply than other kids of the same age.

2. He/she feels hypersensitive being around people, crowds or noise.

3. Your child reacts very strongly to movies, cartoons or dramas.

4. Your child does not seem to fit in well with other children of same age.

5. Your child has an intense feeling of love for animals and plants.

6. Your child has fewer friends than others.

7. He/she trusts people easily and is often fooled.

8. Your child can amaze you by his/her intuitions about others.

9. He/she becomes too sad in others' pains.

10. Staying alone makes your child calm down.

These are the most common signs of an empath, and if the child shows 3 or more of these traits, parents must consider that he/she is one.

A supportive parenting is crucial for an empath in the growing years. It is from the parents that the empath gets acceptance and courage to live with it.

Effective Parenting Strategies for dealing with empaths

Help in minimizing energy loss -- Be a guide to your child and let him release his/her emotional burden. Let him/her cry, share, be angry, and do whatever it takes to feel better. Never judge or scold your child for being over-sensitive. That would draw him/her away from you.

Help your child getting grounded -- Help your child in getting grounded or earthed physically once or twice a week (or as often you need). You can practice physical exercises, games, nature walks, weekend trips or interesting board games. Whatever may be the task, it should captivate the mind of your child and stops him/her from worrying about others. And most important is that parents should also be equally participative in the grounding activities.

Engage the child in creative activities -- Spend time with your child in bringing out his/her creative self. It may be painting, crafts, or music - help your child to find happiness in the things he/she has a passion for. Many studies have shown that empaths who could engage themselves in creative works could better cope with the stresses of the "Empath" life.

Be authoritative as a parent -- If your child is an empath, then you must be careful with how you are dealing with him/her. Authoritative parenting style has been the best parenting strategy known by far to deal with an empath child. Authoritative parenting means you are warm, loving and supportive to the child, but at the same time, you impart values and the sense of right and wrong. Children who are raised by authoritative parents are well adjusted and suffer less from emotional turmoils as they have a clear understanding of what is right or wrong for them.

Protect the child from emotional drain out -- Be watchful what makes your child happy and what makes him/her low. If your child is an empath, then he/she will likely feel exhausted and overwhelmed being around people for long. Take care and keep the child in a comfort zone where he/she can feel calm and not feel overwhelmed. Be the shield unless the child learns to shield himself/herself from getting emotionally carried away.

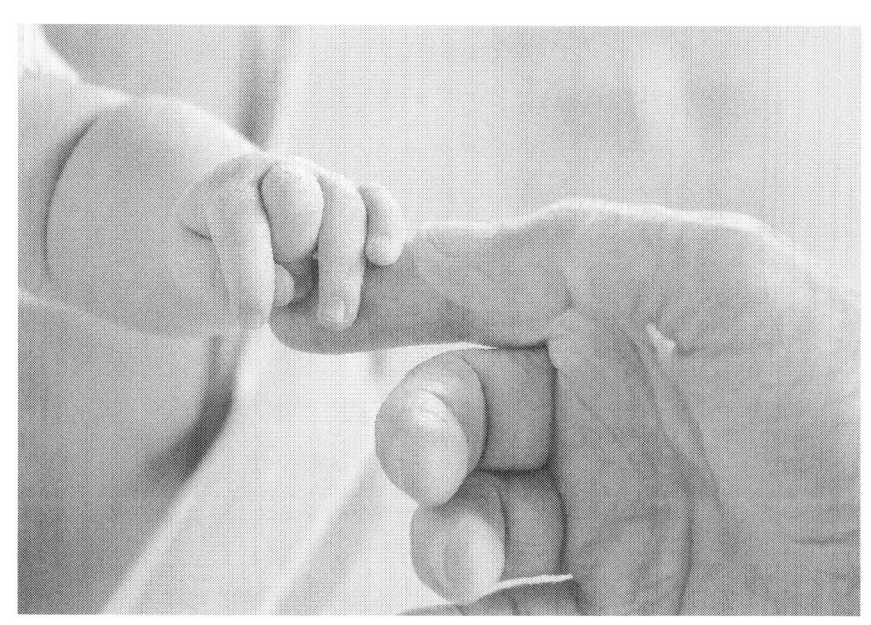

Empath survival
Nuggets to be a skilled Empath

"A sad soul can kill an Empath far quicker than death."
Proverb

1. **Isolate from the energy vampires** -- Recognize the people who drain you out and increase the emotional burden. Being around such people is not healthy for empaths. Preserve your mental energy as much as you can.

2. **Read** -- Perhaps reading is one of the best reliefs for all empaths. They find reading comforting and helps them to divert their minds from the external realities. For those who love to watch movies, you can use that as a stress relief too.

3. **Eat happy** -- Undoubtedly empaths should maintain a healthy diet. But it is always fun to cheat on your diet once a week and grab all that you love to eat. Not that it can remove all worries, but it makes you feel pampered and happy for a while.

4. **Don't let people exploit you** -- Empaths can easily be victims of people who just use their qualities to fulfill their selfish aims. Trust, but do not let others make a fool of you. There are some people out there who just want to take advantage of you.

5. **Imagine** -- Empaths have an imaginative power that is unique to them. With their intuitions and high sensitivity, they can find happiness and sadness in their imaginations. Try imagining all the good things that you want, daydream about the places and situations you want to be in or recollect the old happy memories and bring back the smile on your face. Just close your eyes and indulge yourself into all the beautiful thoughts. As an empath, I myself practice this every time I am alone and trust me, the effect is wondrous.

6. **Be close to yourself** -- Do not let the empath ability detach you from yourself. Even though focusing on the self can seem hard when you are so pressed with the thoughts of other people, it is essential that you are able to connect to your thoughts also. Trust yourself, forgive yourself, pamper yourself and communicate with yourself.

7. **Embrace positivity** -- Even though you may be equally receptive to positive and negative energies, choose positivity. Not only as energy from people around but also choose to think positively. Remember positivity attracts positivity. The more you emit positive vibes,

the more you would receive the same and the less you would be emotionally burdened.

Surviving as an empath may not be an easy task, but you should feel blessed as you are among those chosen ones who can literally "feel" what others are going through. Treasure your qualities as an empath, but remember to set the boundaries wisely.

As Sylvester Mc Nutt (III) had rightly stated, *"Everything I experience hits me deep, raw and intense. As an empath, I feel the energy of myself and others..."*

Conclusion

"I don't hear words, I feel energy. Speak what is true, or I will do it for you."

Empath Proverb.

Empaths can hear everything that people cannot express in words. They can sense the silence, the body movements, gestures, and tone. Surviving as an empath is an emotional experience at all stages. However, the distress is much more when we are unaware of our "empath" self.

The first step towards healthy survival is recognizing yourself as an Empath. That makes much of the struggle easy. The Grounding Techniques, Relationship Skills, and Life Hacks that I have mentioned in this book will help you in the journey of being an empath. Focus on how you can transform energies that you consume and do something productive with that. Learn to vent out and let go of what you cannot control. Communicate as much you want, but do not let others misuse your emotions.

As the beautiful saying goes, _"Sensitivity is your strength, while the mind is in the dark, the heart sees the problem long before."_

Your greatest empath gift is your instinct. No matter how easily you can trust others or feel their pain, never forget to follow what your gut feeling says. Empaths who trust their own instincts are much well-adjusted than others. Remember, you can never heal others if you are broken from within. So step forward in making yourself happy and embrace your blessing as an empath.

Copyright 2018 by Amalia Elle - All rights reserved.

All rights Reserved. No part of this publication or the information in it may be quoted from or reproduced in any form by means such as printing, scanning, photocopying or otherwise without prior written permission of the copyright holder.

Disclaimer and Terms of Use: Effort has been made to ensure that the information in this book is accurate and complete, however, the author and the publisher do not warrant the accuracy of the information, text and graphics contained within the book due to the rapidly changing nature of science, research, known and unknown facts and internet. The Author and the publisher do not hold any responsibility for errors, omissions or contrary interpretation of the subject matter herein. This book is presented solely for motivational and informational purposes only.

Printed in Great Britain
by Amazon